Table Of Contents

Foreward

Introduction

Pursuing Uncomfortable

Lean In and Overcome

Rev. Melissa Ebken

Light Life and Love Ministries®

PURSUING UNCOMFORTABLE

Lean In and Overcome

Cover Design: Tail Chase Marketing

Print ISBN: 9798218551384
Ebook ISBN: 9798218551391

To my family.

Foreward

From the moment I met Melissa, I knew there was something special about her. She seemed to possess a calm, steady strength that pulled me in. As our friendship has grown, I have learned that she has been shaped by moments of courage to face the hardest parts of life with grace, wisdom, and resilience. When she told me she was writing this book, I wasn't surprised. I knew her life experiences would serve as a lighthouse for others.

This book is not just a collection of stories or reflections—it's an invitation. An invitation to look at your own life through a lens of honesty, courage, and vulnerability. It also serves as a support as you work to "overcome the difficult and uncomfortable yuck in your life." Through her words, Melissa shares not only what she's learned but also how she continues to grow through every new challenge. As you read, you'll find yourself reflecting on the times you've been tested, how you've navigated loss and grief, and the ways you can grow in the face of those trials.

In the introduction, Melissa shares a recurring

nightmare that many of us can relate to—running from something unknown. It's a powerful metaphor for how we often respond to fear and anxiety. But she doesn't leave us in that moment of running; she walks us through her journey of learning to stop and face what keeps her up at night. As she does, she brings us along for the ride, reminding us that we, too, can find the strength to confront what we're running from.

The themes of courage, healing, and facing challenges head-on are woven throughout her stories. As Melissa shares the deeply personal experience of grieving the loss of her mother, she invites us into a moment of vulnerability that is both universal and profound. The image of her sitting around the table with her brothers, playing a simple card game, grieving and healing in the same breath, is a testament to the power of human connection. Life, in all its complexity, continues on, and we are left to navigate it with whatever tools we have.

Melissa doesn't shy away from the hard stuff. She's candid about the moments of pain, fear, and sorrow that we all experience, but she's also committed to showing us how to move through those moments. Her own journey is one marked by an unrelenting commitment to growth, even when it would be easier to give in to avoidance or despair. And it's in these real, raw moments that her greatest gift shines through—her ability to offer us not just hope, but a roadmap.

This book is a powerful reminder that healing is an ongoing process, one that requires intentionality, community, and grace. Melissa shares her plan for moving forward after the loss of her mother—one that includes healthy habits, deepening connections, and the willingness to be vulnerable. It's not just a survival plan but a blueprint for living. She goes on to share, "I can do difficult things. I can heal from grief. I can create strategies to overcome obstacles."

At the heart of Melissa's message, we are reminded that we are capable of far more than we often realize, and the journey to heal and grow is one we can all take if we choose to. Her words are both a gentle guide and a strong call to action.

I am honored to know Melissa, and I know that by the time you finish this book, you will feel the same way. She has found her voice. Her words will resonate with you long after you turn the last page, not because they offer easy answers but because they are rooted in truth, courage, and a deep understanding of the human spirit. She shows us that while life will undoubtedly bring challenges, it is also full of opportunities for growth, connection, and love.

This book is a gift, not just because of its wisdom but

because of the love behind it. Dive in with an open mind and heart, and you will find not only inspiration but also the tools to build a life of resilience and joy no matter what comes your way.

-Molly Grisham, Owner and Lead Facilitator at MollyGrisham.com Get Your Lightbulb Moments!

Introduction

The scream caught in my throat. I tried to run, but could barely move, like I was running through deep water. It's about to catch me...

Gasping for air, I bolted awake. Another nightmare. I didn't have them frequently, per se, but often enough. They began innocuously and then something in my dream would morph into something bigger and scary and begin chasing me. I would try to scream and run, unable to do either. Then, I would wake suddenly, my heart thumping in my chest.

These dreams happened more frequently in my younger years, but still lingered in adulthood. If it's true that our dreams are representative of our lives, and are an attempt made by our subconscious to work out or work through our anxieties, then it makes sense to me that they have lessened and mostly dissipated. For much of my life, I ran from what scared me. I have learned to turn and face whatever would cause me fear and anxiety.

In my nightmares, it was always something otherwise harmless that suddenly became big and terrifying. Hmm... , I thought, sitting with my chin in one hand and tapping my pen on a blank journal page with the other, thinking about the dream that had jolted me awake moments earlier. That's an apt metaphor for me. I have a tendency to deny or look away from a problem that makes me anxious. It tends to grow and loom in the back of my mind until I finally deal with it. Once I do, I realize that it wasn't as big and frightening as my fear had made it out to be, and wish I had dispatched with it much sooner.

Reflecting back on my life I recount the times when I courageously faced problems, and other times when I ignored or evaded them. A pattern emerges. I think about the people I pastor and I can see the same pattern in their lives, too. There's tremendous value in confronting our fears, taming our troubles, and getting a little uncomfortable. Time spent worrying, fearing, and avoiding problems, is time added to them. In that extra time, we create unhealthy narratives for ourselves, feeding our inner voice and expressing our lack of ability, smarts, or worth.

Conversely, when we face a difficult problem head-on and overcome it - it feels amazing! Expressions of kudos and positive reinforcement resound throughout our conscious and subconscious mind, empowering us to tackle even bigger issues. We believe we are capable of big things and therefore, we are.

Doesn't it feel gratifying to put a problem behind you? Of course it does! I think we run from major problems because we don't know how to confront them. Maybe we don't know how to start. I wrote this book to encourage you.

You can do difficult things. You are worth the effort. You are more capable and resilient than you think you are. Ultimately, we can overcome the most difficult and impossible situations and experiences - not because of our own strength - but by surrendering our strength and connecting with the still, quiet voice of the Divine within each of us.

In this book, I share how I came to understand how to pursue the uncomfortable instead of running from it and grow towards light, life, and love. I lay out the cornerstones that helped me to process and overcome life's challenges; cornerstones I have seen in the lives of others who grow through their own challenges, too. You can do difficult things. You can overcome difficulties. You can build your resilience. This book will help you.

Chapter 1: The First Stand

I sat criss-cross applesauce, as my son used to say, in the belly of a UH-1H "Huey" Army training helicopter at Fort Rucker, Alabama, staring at an improperly installed cargo hook assembly. We were inside an enormous hangar, with Huey helicopters angle-parked along each wall. The hangar had a glossy gray concrete floor and the walls and rounded ceiling were dark, disappearing in the task lighting that lit the workspaces. Each aircraft was now a trainer, no longer flying, with the long side doors removed to ease access. A careful eye would notice slightly off-color spots along the body and tail of the aircraft where "bondo" had been applied, repairing damage suffered in combat. Each aircraft in that hangar had a story to tell of its heroic service. They now served as trainers, each with a student inside working on a task to become competent in helicopter maintenance and repair.

I had just finished installing the cargo hook assembly as my last test in the school. If you imagine a helicopter flying and extending a hook downward to retrieve a person or piece of equipment, that hook assembly was what I had just installed. Well, sort of. It was backward. I had installed it with the clasp of the hook facing to the rear of the helicopter instead of to the front. My dilemma was that this failed attempt would prevent me from achieving my goal.

I was in AIT, Advanced Individual Training. When a recruit joins the Army, he or she goes to Basic Training to learn how to become a soldier. After Basic Training, that soldier goes to AIT to receive specialized training for the job he or she will do in the Army. I was learning how to repair and maintain a helicopter; my job with the Illinois Army National Guard. I was about to fail the cargo hook assembly installation task. I had taken an hour and a half of my allotted two hours to install it *incorrectly,* so my confidence in getting it installed *correctly* in half an hour was low. However, we had two opportunities to pass this test, so though I would not pass on the first attempt, I would pass the second and complete the course. I would graduate and move on in my Army National Guard career. However - and this is a big "however" - if I did not pass it on the first attempt, I would not be eligible to be the Honor Graduate of the program. Becoming an Honor Graduate was at stake for me, and it was really dang important.

For you to understand why it mattered so much to me, I need to back up to the beginning of that summer. On June 6, 1989, I had just graduated high school and had flown into Ft. Rucker, Alabama to begin AIT. I arrived late at night and was dropped off at the barracks, where I could catch a few hours' sleep before reporting for training the following morning. Early the next morning, with the barracks to our back, five of us, newly arrived soldiers, stood shoulder to shoulder on the hot asphalt as we "toed the line." We faced a formation of soldiers from Company C, the helicopter maintenance training company for the UH-1H "Huey" helicopter. We didn't stand there very long. Drill sergeants descended upon us like lions capturing their prey. Immediately we dropped to the sizzling pavement, trying to squeeze out as many pushups as possible and fast.

I thought back to Basic Training the previous summer and how that experience was scary and difficult. It quickly became clear that this would be next-level scary and difficult, eclipsing anything I encountered in Basic Training. In the middle of all the yelling from the drill sergeants and my heart thumping in my ears, I heard a voice - a still small voice from inside. It said, "This is what you asked for. Do you think you can do it?"

I had a reason to join the National Guard. I was the youngest of three kids - the only daughter. I had a lot of brains and goals in life, but I didn't have the wherewithal spirit to conquer obstacles and accomplish those goals. I had always defaulted to others in difficult situations. In moments when other kids taunted me or picked on me, I just accepted it and withdrew as quickly as I could. I wanted to stand my ground, express myself, and defend myself. I joined the Illinois Army National Guard, thinking that would help. I was seventeen, a junior in high school, and my parents had to sign papers to allow me to enlist.

I went to basic training that summer, between my junior and senior years of high school in Ft. Jackson, South Carolina. If you were not alive in the summer of 1988, or do not remember that summer, there was a drought. And it was hot. So. Very. Hot. I thought that was the big test. It's basic training, right? That's supposed to be *the big deal.* I completed basic training and felt like a big shot. I returned home to complete my senior year of high school, and after graduation, I got on a plane to Ft. Rucker, Alabama, to attend AIT and learn to fix Hueys.

AIT was supposed to be the checkbox on my way to the other things I planned. Go to college and conquer the world as a renowned biologist. To be honest, I hadn't given AIT much thought. AIT is a step down from Basic Training, in that it's a little looser environment and you have more freedoms and fewer restrictions. The good folks at Ft. Rucker, in the UH-1H maintenance training Company C, however, did not get that memo. Their motto was "Attention To Detail." They said things, like "We are the Company that sets the standard." If you have been in the service, you understand what kind of fresh Hell being "The Company That Sets The Standard" entails.

Apparently, when you ask the universe for something, it has to make a big deal about it and it keeps popping up and asking you, "Are you sure? Is this what you *REALLY* want?" As I did push-up after push-up in the hot Alabama sun, it asked me: "Are you going to choose to find the strength within yourself?" Gritting my teeth against the searing heat of the asphalt, I said, "Yes. I'm going to find my strength!" Immediately in my gut, I sensed that choosing to find the strength within myself meant I had one of two choices. Either I would fail miserably and forget about serving in the IL Army National Guard. Or I would come out on top and be the Honor Graduate in this AIT experience. I needed to decide quickly which it was going to be.

I decided I was going to come out on top.

The universe said, "Okay! Do it." What I didn't realize at that tender young age was that the universe would continue to require clarity throughout my time in AIT.

AIT lasted more than those first difficult minutes. Twelve weeks stretched before me, and my future as a biologist felt like a million miles away. Repeatedly, I would confront another level of difficulty.

There was one other woman in the training company of around fifty. She was a few weeks ahead of me in the training. Every week, some in the company would graduate and others would arrive and begin their training. We began each morning with physical training (PT). Three to five times a week we would run as a company. Guess who got to set the running pace? Not me. Not the other woman, either. We ran at a pace that was comfortable-to-challenging for the guys, which meant it was challenging to are you kidding me, for me. Admittedly, it is a little different when you run in a pack. With people on all sides, I mainly had to keep my legs and lungs operating. This was good since most of the time I could only see spots. I often couldn't feel much of my body, but I kept my legs and lungs going. The budding biologist in me seriously wondered if my lungs could burn through my chest and out of my body. Again, the Universe popped in and said, "How about now? Can you find the strength within yourself?" I wanted to quit. I wanted to fall by the wayside, walk and catch my breath. Or maybe collapse. Some guys did fall out of the runs from time to time. They paid mightily for it. I kept on.

An Army post is a city unto itself. Main and side roads direct traffic to their intended destinations. There are "business" zones with office buildings where people work and "private" zones with housing. Each post has a mall called PX, short for Post Exchange. Most posts have schools, grocery stores, recreation centers, and other facilities needed to support community life. Each morning, reveille plays as a soldier raises the U.S. flag in front of the post headquarters. All soldiers out-of-doors stop and come to attention. Each evening, retreat (taps) plays as the post flag lowers, and again all soldiers out-of-doors stop and come to attention.

On a training post, drill sergeants march their platoons from location to location, calling out a cadence and the platoon responds. After morning PT, our drill sergeant would march us across the post to the school inside the hangar, and release us into the charge of those running the school. Here, we learned all about the UH-1H helicopter. The first two weeks were classroom work. We learned how to keep a logbook, maintain maintenance records, and learned to read and use the maintenance instruction manuals.

In the following weeks, we cycled through the various levels of training: learning about the fuel system, the electric system, the power plant, etc. A lot of this was new to me, not having a background in mechanics, but I learned the tasks and passed each level with no failed attempts. We had two chances at each task they tested us on, but it was important to me I pass on the first because I was determined to be the Honor Graduate. One failed attempt and I wouldn't qualify. I was going to come out on top. I was finding my groove and saw a path through this, though the end was still many weeks away.

But the universe hadn't finished with me yet.

It was 1989. Some didn't want me, a woman, to be there in the company of men training to be a helicopter mechanic, let alone to excel in my training. Thus, at 18, I had my first *#metoo* moment. The experience (experiences actually) was humiliating. I didn't know what to do about my situation, but I knew what I *would not* do. I feared my decision would get me booted, but I knew my limits - I would not *find strength within myself* if I *gave up myself*. At 18, I didn't have the vocabulary or wisdom to articulate that sentiment, but I knew a line I was not willing to cross. I would not be forced to use my body as capital.

Days later, as the threats and harassment continued, we were back in our company area, and I was in the supply room with some others, sweeping and tidying up. I was oblivious to the others, alone with my thoughts, mulling over my choices and trying to understand the consequences. I believed that if I spoke up, no one would believe me and I would get punished, and ultimately kicked out. The Army doesn't like people who buck the system, right?

I needed more information. I played it cool. I casually approached the supply sergeant and asked him, "If something happens at the school, do we use the chain of command at the school or do we use the chain of command here in our Company?" Just a simple question, no big deal.

8

The Army is big on the chain of command, and I was merely looking for clarity. It was research.

Either Sgt. Larson had mind-reading abilities, or I wasn't as cool as I thought. He took a look at me, then ordered everyone out of the supply room, closed the door, set a chair out in front of him, and told me to spill it (so much for his mind-reading abilities). I wasn't ready to talk about it yet. It was complex and awful and I like to process things in my mind first and understand consequences before I act, especially when the stakes are high. But there we were, so I told him the story. He listened without saying a word and sent me to the Mess Hall to eat supper with the rest of the company. Now things were beyond my control and I was afraid of what would happen next.

I had hardly made it through the chow line with my tray when someone came and said I was to report to the First Sergeant's office immediately.

Gulp. Soon enough, I would know how alone I would be in this situation, and whether I would even have a future here.

If you've not been in the Army, you need to know that the First Sergeant is in charge. Yes, there's a company commander - usually a captain, but the captain doesn't interact with the company often. The First Sergeant, though, is the boss. This is who runs things. This is the one who holds the power for and over the soldiers in the company. Our First Sergeant was FIERCE. He demanded the best - the absolute best - from the soldiers in his command and settled for nothing less. He praised us when we delivered it. He had our absolute trust and loyalty. We would have marched into any situation behind him.

I was terrified as I walked to his office. He was a scary guy. I had immense loyalty to and respect for him, but I did not know how far his loyalty and respect extended to those in his command. He lavished his approval on us when we continued to meet the top bar he set for us. But would he view *me* as the problem or the poor behavior of the instructor at the school as the problem? Though I was young, I knew how the world worked, and what the easiest course of action would be for him.

I reported to his office and saw a furious man. I could feel the heat of his anger and could almost see the smoke coming from his ears. I braced myself. As I took in more of the scene, I saw him pacing and ranting, "Nobody messes with *my* soldiers! Nobody!" I was shaking inside.

He asked me to tell him my story. I *hated* telling the story. When I finished, he assured me the instructor would be gone. I believed him and exhaled a little. I had the support of my company, anyway. What would happen at the school was yet to be seen.

When we arrived at the school the next morning the instructor was gone. The other instructors pulled me aside and said I had nothing to fear from them. They assured me that what the other instructor did was wrong and I should not mistake them for him. Ok, another breath.

The leadership at the school, however, presented a different problem. It felt like they wanted me gone. Legally, they had to accept me there. But they now, with this incident, had a mark against them. In subtle ways, they did what they could to disrupt my training and make passing each level more difficult. They would pull me out of instruction to give a report. They often "lost" reports and needed to make new ones. I believed they used these excuses to pull me out and disrupt my training. Each time they did, I would have to face a higher-ranking officer in a fancier office full of men and tell my story in excruciating detail. It was intimidating. Humiliating. Embarrassing. I hated telling the story. I felt defenseless and small. Even though I hadn't submitted to my aggressor's direct attempts, he found creative ways to embarrass and humiliate me in front of the others in my company. My grown-up body was still new to me and I was far from comfortable in my skin. I didn't know how to handle such attention. Talking about all of it repeatedly, in a room full of men who had authority over me was another level of trauma.

The guys in my platoon saw what was happening and stood by me. They encouraged me to fight it and they filed reports, too. I would not have had this experience without their support. It isn't logical, but feelings of shame loomed large, even though there was no reason to feel shame. I had done nothing wrong. And yet... I think many women feel this too. It's difficult to put words to, but it weighs significantly in situations of harassment and abuse.

My company mates came through for me. In the evenings, they would talk me through what I had missed, and I would go to the learning center across the street and practice the tasks I needed to learn. Those were arduous weeks. They almost broke me. I felt beaten and thought about quitting. My family wanted to come down and help me (rescue me) as they always had and I wanted to let them. But, I didn't. As long as I could keep going, I planned to keep going.

In the quietness of those nights, lying awake, silently weeping in the darkness, I knew this was a big test, and I wanted to pass it. By far, it was the hardest time of my life. Nobody could walk this path for me. It was up to me. I knew I needed to get through this. If I could pull through all of this, not only would I be confident in my ability to find the strength I needed within, but I could face difficult things. I could overcome hardship. I could build a life I wanted instead of quietly accepting what came my way.

When you do something impossible, the world feels different. In many ways, Army training is a series of doing impossible things. Scale that wall. Complete this days-long task in one afternoon. One thing after another taught us that not only could we do hard things, but when we pulled together, we could do seemingly impossible things. But this situation felt too big for me.

I hung in there and kept going. I intentionally quit focusing on the enormity of the situation. Instead, I focused on what was in front of me, moment to moment, completing a task and moving to the next. I had to force my brain to follow what my mind and soul needed. This change of mindset helped tremendously. My body was fitter than it had ever been, and my psyche, though fragile, was getting stronger each day. Days passed, and the finish line was edging closer. My goal began to feel possible.

Until I was sitting criss-cross applesauce in the belly of that helicopter, looking at the cargo hook assembly that I installed backward.

Seriously?

After all that I had overcome, all that I had endured, all the growth that I had developed - this was what would take me down?

The cargo hook installation isn't difficult cognitively, actually, it's simple. The difficulty lies in stretching the powerful springs upward, holding them in place, and bolting the assembly on a spindle in just the right spot. It takes a lot of strength to stretch it up, hold it in place, and torque it down without it slipping. We had to attach it within an inch of tolerance and tighten it to a specified torque. I had spent an hour and a half wrestling with it and I was exhausted. So of course, the universe came be-bopping back in, saying, "What about now? What are you going to do? Are you going to settle? Ready to give up?"

It was tempting. I can't tell you how tempting it was. I could concede this attempt, try it again, pass the task, finish the training, and get on with my future. I didn't *have* to be the honor grad, I just needed to graduate.

This was the last task in our maintenance training. I couldn't leave it as it was. I couldn't give up - not after everything.

I released it.

I loosened the attaching hardware, TURNED THE DANG THING THE RIGHT WAY, said a prayer, and got on with it.

I repositioned myself to leverage more strength for one last attempt. As I did, I realized I could slide my legs through and beneath the springs and use my legs to extend the springs upward and hold them in position. This allowed me to use both my hands to tighten down and torque the assembly into place.

Brilliant!

And, done.

Correctly.

In time.

I finally convinced the universe that I had learned what I wanted to learn and it gave me the inspiration I needed. It's as if that final refusal to give up released a lock and a door opened.

"Thank you, God!"

At that moment, I finally realized that, all along, it was God and not some disembodied challenger in the universe who was present and asked me if I was finding what I wanted. All that time, I had been praying and crying out - wanting God and God's strength and comfort - and feeling as though I was forgotten, left alone to face it all. I finally realized that it was God all along. No devil was trying to trap me. God had heard my prayer all those years for something more in my life - to be stronger, to express myself, and to stand up for myself and others. God knew the plans for me and the strength I would need to live and fulfill them. God was with me every step. It was God asking me if this was what I wanted. It was God who guided me to dig deep and trust the strength within. What I needed to learn, was the strength I had been searching for wasn't my strength at all, though it was within me.

Friend, God is our very core. *(You may call it something different - you may call upon God by another name. You may refer to that LOVING-ENERGY-FORCE as Higher Power, Spirit, Source, or Something Else. I use God.)* I learned and continue to learn, that God is not an OUT THERE go-and-find-it fixer. God is an IN-HERE presence within each of us. The problem is, that we cover that divine presence within us with a lot of ego and other garbage. When we peel all that other stuff away and finish with our own reasoning, excuses, and strength, and have nothing left to show for ourselves; we finally look to the depths of our being. There, we find God.

It was done. I installed the cargo hook assembly correctly and within the time allotted. This was the last task. One other soldier and I were the only ones qualified to become an Honor Graduate. We both needed to complete this task successfully to qualify. If we both did, I would have the edge as my scores in other areas were higher. When I torqued down that assembly correctly, I sealed it. I was the Honor Graduate.

I could breathe. The mountain was gone. It was somewhere behind me.

The graduation was fantastic. I will never forget how I felt as I received my diploma and pinned my wings to my uniform. And get this - I received an Army Achievement Medal! The very folks who tried to impede my progress at the school were the ones who had the duty to pin it on me. Friend, I *savored* that moment. What can I say, I'm still a work in progress. :)

Chapter 2: Building Faith

Getting my wings was more than the pin on my uniform and the authorization to work on the UH-1H Army helicopter. I learned that a strength greater than my own lives within me through that experience. At 18, it was a difficult concept to grasp. Even now, north of fifty, that knowledge astounds and humbles me. Who am I that God would dwell so intimately? Who am I that God would inspire, encourage, challenge, refine, and send?

In her book *A Return To Love*, Marianne Williamson writes,

> *"Our deepest fear is not that we are inadequate. Our deepest fear is that we are powerful beyond measure. It is our light, not our darkness that most frightens us. We ask ourselves, Who am I to be brilliant, gorgeous, talented, fabulous? Actually, who are you not to be? You are a child of God. Your playing small does not serve the world. There is nothing enlightened about shrinking so that other people won't feel insecure around you. We are all meant to shine, as children do. We were born to make manifest the glory of God that is within us. It's*

not just in some of us; it's in everyone. And as we let our own light shine, we unconsciously give other people permission to do the same. As we are liberated from our own fear, our presence automatically liberates others."[1]

I think she nailed it. It's a lot easier to believe our faults, isn't it? Do you have that voice that tells you that you're not good/smart/educated/qualified enough to be or do what you're thinking about being or doing? Yeah, me too. It's a pain in the neck. I won't let that voice have the last word. I don't want you to let that voice influence you, either. That's the big lesson I learned in AIT. The voice isn't the only voice that speaks, though it often speaks the loudest. I have learned that when I stop listening to it, quiet my soul, and turn down the volume, a much better voice comes in the silence. It takes a while to "tune into" that voice because many layers cover it. My ego, my education, my reason, my excuses, my experience, my accomplishments, my doubts, my failures, my hopes, my dreams, my constructs of what should and should not be in this world; all these things cover that still, small voice within that is God.

It's easy to mistake any of these layers for God's wisdom, and I often do. Or, I knowingly accept my wisdom

---

[1] Marianne Williamson, *A Return To Love* (Harper Collins: 1992), 165

as good enough. Sometimes it is. However, to hear the voice of the Spirit I know as God requires me to delve beneath all the layers that cover it. That's the hard part. With time and practice, we can cultivate a prayer or meditation discipline that gives us access to cut through those layers to the voice of wisdom from within. But, as I discovered in AIT, initially cutting through those layers involves struggle and even failure.

We find God in our mess. The problem is that we are not wired to set aside our egos, knowledge, and experience and rely on the counter-cultural voice speaking from our depths. We cling tightly to them. Struggle jettisons our iron grip on our accomplishments and we feel rotten and exposed, maybe even embarrassed. Access to true wisdom, the clear voice of God within each of us, becomes ever more accessible to us in the darkness of those experiences and redeems them. What was ugly or disrupted can become beautifully whole. Fr. Richard Rohr delves into this topic in his book *Falling Upward: A Spirituality for the Two Halves of Life*. In it, he describes how the experience of falling, or failing, can actually be a falling upward. The experience of falling, or failing, lays aside the things we look to for wisdom and even authority, which only shield us from the Wisdom we seek. This falling leads us beyond our own understanding, ego, and experience and into a deeper and more substantial presence of God where there is a greater potential for healing and wellness.[2]

Initially, this may sound like bad news. I think it's good news. I think it's *very* good news. The persistent message in Scripture is that God's love is not something we earn. It's not something we achieve through our hard work and efforts. It's not something we have because of our good deeds. God's love is a gift given to us graciously and mercifully. It is accessible to each of us, as we find it at the very core of our being. God created humanity and called it good. Then, God breathed into the human and a relationship was born. The very essence of God is in the air we draw into our bodies. God is at our core and available to each of us. We encounter this presence within, not in our *doing*, but in our *undoing*. In other words, when we make a royal mess of things, we have greater access to God and God's mercy, grace, and Wisdom.

Each of us experiences our undoing throughout life. We fail. We make mistakes and face impossible situations and experiences. We grieve, struggle, and doubt. We chase our demons and desperately grasp for anything that offers hope. Ultimately, bereft of any other help or hope, we turn to God and find a love and peace that transcends our despair. It

---

[2] Fr. Richard Rohr, *Falling Upward: A Spirituality for the Two Halves of Life* (Jossey-Bass: 2011) Book description

was with us the entire time, but now we know it. Instead of answers, we have better questions. We receive peace and acceptance as we are in our incompleteness. We discover we are whole and wholly loved. This is the Good News. It is the Gospel. This is redemption in whatever spiritual or religious language you speak.

Jean Piaget did seminal work on how we grow and develop cognitively. You may also be familiar with Abraham Maslow and his Hierarchy Of Needs, which outlines what a person needs to achieve self-actualization.[3] James Fowler built upon Piaget's and Maslow's work and posited his seminal work about how we grow and develop faith. The work of each is taught broadly and provides a basic understanding of how our minds, emotions, and faith develop.

From Piaget's work, we learn that at around twelve years of age, we gain the ability to think abstractly, which opens up the possibility of a dynamic faith in God.[4] This leads us to the potential found in Faith Stages 3 and beyond, according to Fowler's work in faith and religious

---

[3] Mcleod, Saul, PhD. "Maslow's Hierarchy Of Needs." *Simply Psychology*, Jan. 2024, https://www.simplypsychology.org/maslow.html

[4] Lewis, Charlie, and Jeremy I.M. Carpendale. "Piaget's Stages of Cognitive Development Explained." *Child & Family Blog*, Oct. 2018, https://childandfamilyblog.com/piaget-stages-cognitive-development/?gclid=Cj wKCAiA7vWcBhBUEiwAXieItmjM1CWZv3YKKOosfjGrZYX8UJApwRoc_lOYUT 1CSrY-DpALTAra_hoCrsIQAvD_BwE.

development.[5] *(These stages Fowler describes are not automatic; many do not develop past Stage 3, for instance. The ages associated with each stage are a general guide to when that stage becomes available to an individual to manifest in his or her life.)* The earliest stages concern how we develop as children. Please see the reference below for a description of the early stages of faith development. I'm jumping ahead to Stage 3 for our discussion here, which becomes available around age 12.

The development of an individual's spiritual identity in relationship to a religious institution characterizes stage 3. I am Christian. I am Jewish. I am Muslim. This is broadly true throughout the many cultures and traditions in our world. This is the age that many cultures enact rites of passage. In my tradition, which is Christian, this is the age that we baptize or confirm those raised in the faith. Other traditions practice rites of passage around this age as well.[6]

Struggle characterizes stage 4 of Fowler's Stages of Faith. Generally, from our mid-twenties to late thirties, we grow out of the faith of our childhood when/if that faith container cannot reconcile our faith and experiences. This is a difficult time and often people in this stage of faith and life

---

[5] Armstrong, Thomas. "The Stages of Faith According to James W. Fowler." *American Institute For Learning and Human Development*, 12 June 2020, https://www.institute4learning.com/2020/06/12/the-stages-of-faith-according-to-james-w-fowler/.

[6] Ibid.

express a lot of doubt and don't practice their faith, or do so with less assuredness. This age often sees a lot of hardship, struggle, and distress. Many stay in this stage and don't progress in their faith development beyond this state of doubt. [7] Hmm... ever wonder why we don't see many twenty-somethings in our churches? Pray for them. They are in a difficult stage of faith development.

Stage 5 is characterized by a person's understanding that there aren't always answers. They have plumbed the depths of doubt and the insufficiency of their younger faith (stage 4), and found their way to a deeper understanding. Sometimes the questions are more interesting than any answer could be. One who reaches this stage of faith knows that there is a Presence beyond our experience, that all people are worthy of compassion, and sometimes we have to live with paradox. Truth includes and lies beyond any articulated faith statement. And this is enough. We can have peace and purpose without having all knowledge. [8]

This Stage 5 awareness is what I describe in this book that we attain when we, as Richard Rohr would say, "fall upward." I experienced a brief glimpse of this possibility that summer in Ft. Rucker, and years later, after many struggles and doubts, would find my way to embrace it in my life. A

---

[7] Ibid.
[8] Ibid.

richness of spiritual experience is available at this point in life. It's what I invite you to consider as we move through this book together and discuss how faith speaks to us and sustains us when we pursue the uncomfortable - when we lean into the garbage and yuck of this life and emerge with a greater understanding of ourselves and the God we know to be as close and intimate as the air we draw into our bodies. The reward of going through something that knocks you off of your foundation is this richness of relationship with God.

When we face adversity, we need our faith and access to the indwelling wisdom of God at our core. The difficulty is we do not feel loyal. Life's challenges have knocked us off our foundation and we no longer know how to stand firm in our beliefs. The dilemma, is how do we draw upon our faith when we do not feel faithful?

Let's approach this from another angle. Are you married? If so, you know there are moments when you do not like your spouse. However, you love him or her profoundly. The love you have, which transcends that moment, guides your actions and you engage in the difficulty before you accordingly. You won't destroy the love and commitment you share over this moment of irritation. Do you have children? If so, you know there are moments when love is not the emotion bubbling to the top. Kids can act like stinky, rotten turds. But you love them. So much. Your love for them transcends the emotion you feel at the moment and guides you as you interact with their loveliness.

In each of these examples, your actions are not based on what you *feel*, but upon what you **know** to be true through and beyond the current moment. You choose to let what you **know** to guide your actions rather than letting your emotions take charge. This is a good definition of maturity. It's also an excellent description of emotional intelligence, self-awareness, and self-differentiation. Spiritual and emotional maturity are two sides of the same coin. To be spiritually mature, we must also be emotionally mature. Spiritual and emotional growth are two sides of the same coin.

Faith is no exception. Moving forward based on what you **know** to be true and transcends the moment, rather than on what you *feel*, is an apt description of faith. Once you **know** God at your core - an essential aspect of your being - that knowledge transcends what you *feel* amid adversity. I may feel sad today, but I know that feeling is transitory. When you find yourself in a moment and can't see or feel the wisdom, truth, joy, hope, and abundance; let your **knowing** guide your actions. Faith trusts that there's more to the story than what we see. Often, what feels like an ending may actually be a beginning. We usually can't see that as it unfolds, unfortunately. We become aware of it retrospectively.

Spiritual practices are powerful because they keep you attuned to the knowing. When you become lost in your struggles, there's a temptation to forget what you **know** to be true. Spiritual practices ground you and remind you there's so much more than what is visible. Read the sacred texts. Pray the prayers. Do the meditations. Listen to the stories of others. Lean into the truth that you **know** to be eternal. Then, when you struggle, face uncertainty, and stand before an impassable mountain, the knowing will guide you. You want a life that is built upon eternal truths, not one that is built upon momentary glimpses and feelings. My purpose in sharing this book with you, beloved, is to remind you that you can do this. I know you can because I know the One who dwells at the center of your being.

Chapter 3: An Uncomfortable Truth

"Don't ever sing in public again!" Those words hit me like a ton of bricks and affected my life more than I'd like to admit. I was in choir in high school. As I implied earlier, I was painfully shy and mostly wanted to blend in. The problem was, I did things that required me to stand out and my interests required me to "put myself out there," so to speak. I'm still not sure why I joined the chorus. I don't have a beautiful voice, but I do enjoy singing. Mostly, I hid out in the alto section, though I have a soprano voice.

It came time for the annual contest, where band and chorus members prepared pieces to perform for a judge. I prepared a saxophone solo in band and a voice solo in chorus. I did well on the saxophone performance but struggled with nerves in my voice solo. Looking back, it makes sense - I hadn't found my voice yet; in any sense of the word. I was so nervous, and I let my nerves get the best of me. I squeaked out my song. Without the confident "oomph" to power it, it fell flat. Literally, my voice was flat, and, thus, I received a low score. The following week at school, my chorus instructor reviewed the performance with me and my low score. He was displeased, and told me, "Don't ever sing in public again!"

It's funny how things stick with you. Some critiques can roll right off your back and you adjust and never consider it again. Others have sticking power. I am sure I received hundreds of critiques throughout my time in school. I had to, right? Save this one, I don't remember any of them. I see now why this one stuck with me; I was struggling to find my voice and place in the world and this critique told me to shut down my voice.

There was another incident of consequence in my junior year of high school. Many students banded together for a cause that didn't seem right to me. In fact, it felt deliberately untrue and hurtful. They asked me to sign a petition, and I did, going along and blending in, as was my pattern. After thinking about it, I reconsidered and took a stand, clarifying my voice in the matter. I was alone on my stand. I made a mistake signing the petition without thinking. Lesson learned. Others mistreated me for my change of heart. It was an awful year and I suffered a lot. I spoke before finding my voice. When I did, it did not go well. This pattern kept coming up in many aspects of my life. When the opportunity to join the National Guard presented itself, I was glad I chose it.

My life has been a series of events around my finding and claiming my voice, and then using it to build up myself and others. Given this insight now, I can look back and see why my music teacher's critique stung so badly; it hit my core struggle. It seems silly that this proverbial monkey on my back has been so troublesome over the years, but it has. My life choices have led me to be in front of people as we sing together. Every Sunday in worship, we sing and I am in front with no place to hide. And each Sunday as we sing, a part of me shrinks back and inward into myself.

It all came to a head during a Christmas Eve service. Our organist was going to be out of town, so we recorded all the accompaniment ahead of time and I put it into the slide presentation for the service. Many elements of the service relied on technology and my A/V guy (my husband) and I tested all of it the day before, from beginning to end. It was seamless. Technology, though, has a will of its own. The following evening, it didn't cooperate. None of the accompaniment played. The slide came up; I turned the volume up, and no sound came out. Well, that's not true - some slides played the first second of the music and then stopped. I am not kidding you. Some slides played nothing at all. On the bright side, they were familiar Christmas songs that we all knew well. Terrifying side - I had to start and lead the singing. Ninety-nine percent of me wanted to run into my office and cry. The other one percent - THANK YOU JESUS - took charge and boycotted crying on Christmas.

It was time to lean into this ordeal and overcome it. I made a plan, found the people I needed, addressed my emotions concerning this issue, and changed my mindset. Making a plan, finding your people, addressing your emotions, and adopting a healthy mindset are the four cornerstones of dealing with adversity or any kind of challenge; be they mountainous or molehill-ish. I learned this in AIT at 18, and have experienced it repeatedly throughout my life as difficult things have popped up. I've also seen it while walking with others through their struggles in twenty-five-plus years of ministry. In the coming chapters, we will look at each of these cornerstones.

Chapter 4: Make a Plan

Let's get to it. The purpose of this book is to support you in overcoming the difficult and uncomfortable yuck in your life, and this section gives you the formula to do it.

This chapter is about making a plan. Life comes at us fast. While it can be full of mundane, ordinary days, it can surprise us with beautiful, glory-filled moments. Life also presents us with problems, challenges, and grief. Any of these can cripple us for a time. You have your own story of challenges and core struggles. Can you remember something from your childhood that still overwhelms you occasionally? Are you facing something difficult or terrifying in your life? There's no end to difficulties and challenges. I set a timer for three minutes and wrote a list of them. Here's what I wrote:

- losing a pet
- completing college
- getting married, divorced, remarried
- having children
- buying/building/selling a home
- moving/relocating
- ending a relationship
- getting a scary diagnosis
- starting a new job

- getting fired or laid off
- starting/owning a business
- acquiring new skills
- engaging in a new hobby
- Therapy
- Retirement
- unexpected life changes
- losing: a spouse, parents, job, financial position, confidence, child, memory, house & belongings, or friendships.

There is no end to the difficulties and adversity we face in life. This is not an exhaustive list. I could fill pages with the challenges we face. This does not even consider the challenges faced by other races, nationalities, and socio-political difficulties. It doesn't include problems of class struggle, addiction, and incarceration. The list of struggles one might face in life is endless.

What matters, dear reader, is the struggle *you* face. What is in front of you, *right now*, that scares you?

Life is full of struggles, and how we face them is a testament to our strength and resilience. Whether it's small daily struggles or larger, more long-term issues, we all have challenges that we must confront to move forward.

Do you struggle to balance your personal and professional life? Do you push yourself too much and find it difficult to take the time to care for yourself? If you're always trying to juggle work, family, kids' activities, and your personal life, then you know it's hard to make time for everything. You may stay up late at night, just scrolling through your phone because it's the only time you have to unwind and enjoy some time alone. This can be mentally and physically draining and makes it difficult to find the motivation to keep going.

Perhaps you struggle with self-doubt. If you are someone who always strives to achieve, it's easy to feel like you're not good enough or don't belong. This can be incredibly discouraging and makes it hard to stay motivated and keep pushing forward. It's important to remember that everyone struggles with self-doubt and that it's okay to make mistakes and not be perfect.

Finally, you may struggle to find purpose and meaning in life. It's hard to stay positive and committed to your life when you don't feel you're making a difference. It's important to remember that even small acts of kindness can have a big impact and we can all make a difference in our unique ways.

We can overcome any struggle we face with the right mindset and support. Life is full of challenges, but it's also full of opportunities and possibilities. It's up to us to make the most of them.

Whatever your struggle is, the first cornerstone to overcome it is to make a plan. I use the word cornerstone instead of step because these four cornerstones don't come in order, necessarily. They unfold together and interweave throughout the process. However, it's important to sit down and make a plan so you know where the finish line is. When will there be a checkered flag and screaming fans to spray the champagne at you or to dump the Gatorade over your head? I jest, but it is important to define where the finish point is, even when, maybe especially when, it's an intangible personal growth goal. Sometimes, the finish line will be obvious. If experiencing a health crisis, or buying/selling a home, the finish line is clearer. If your pursuit is more nebulous, consider what its completion might look like.

Once you identify the source of adversity and know where the finish line is, assess the situation and determine what needs to be done to get there. This may involve seeking professional help or advice from family and friends (more on this later). It is also important to determine what resources are available to assist you. What will you need to get from point A to point B?

The next step is to create a plan of action. This plan should include short-term and long-term goals. Short-term goals should focus on immediate needs, such as finding a job, getting a loan, or finding the right professional; while long-term goals should focus on the bigger picture. It is also important to set realistic goals and timelines to ensure success.

Once the plan is in place, it is important to act. This may involve seeking resources or taking small steps to progress toward the goals.

Finally, it is important to remember that adversity is a part of life and that it is possible to overcome it. Having a plan helps to ensure a successful outcome, but it's also important to remain flexible and open to new solutions. (Don't forget to stay positive and trust that your difficult situation can improve!)

My dear friend Molly Grisham shares her story about leaving the position of a college soccer coach and starting her own consulting business. The following includes excerpts from an interview I conducted with Molly on November 23, 2021.[9]

Molly:

I spent almost 20 years teaching and coaching, the last part as a full time college coach. I had sensed for a while that that was probably ending, that there was something else out there for me. One door closing and another door opening at the same time. And I think the

---

[9] Molly Griesheim, interview by Melissa Ebken, November 23, 2021.

challenge for me was I wanted those two things to align and happen at the exact same time. So I want this door to close, as this door opened. And then that would be a sign that this is exactly how it's supposed to be. I knew that what I loved about coaching and teaching was developing my players as people. And that was becoming such a small percentage of my job description. Much of my time was fundraising and recruiting, alumni and admissions tours, and compliance meetings and budget meetings. When do I get to do the thing that I feel like I'm supposed to be doing which is helping these 18 to 22 year olds become better humans and grow up? When is that a priority in my list of daily tasks?

I really began to wonder, and two things happened at the same time. One was, how do I just make that a priority in my day to day job? What can I let go of? How can I force that if my boss isn't going to say it's a priority? How do I make it a priority? And so I did that and really found that's where the life was for me. That was in line with who I am and how I'm supposed to navigate the world. So making that a priority was a clear indicator to me of the path I needed to move in.

At the same time, I'm wrestling with this question of, "Is it possible that that's all I could do? What does my world look like in that scenario? How do I create a world where that's the focus of what I do? That really planted a seed for *me of maybe college coaching was a season of my life, but not the totality of my life. Maybe it gave me a chance to understand what I love doing and test the waters kind of in a safe environment. And maybe I needed to step into something else. I felt like a door was closing and a door was opening all at the same time.*

You see things so clearly when you are on the other side of it. I felt like, in the moment, I needed all these things to align, and that would tell me it was right. That alignment would justify my decision. I needed permission from someone to do this. And now I can look back and say like, sometimes in life, you just want to do something. And that's reason enough. I want to spend my life pouring into people. I don't need all the stars to align. I don't need the shooting stars outside my window every day to say yes, yes, yes. Do this. Sometimes the "yes" is just in that's what I want to do. And so I started journaling on this journey to feel more of: "Is knowing what I want enough permission?" and less of, "Have all the pieces aligned?" Maybe I just want to do this new thing. And that's okay.

Melissa:

Have there been days when you were terrified? Because things weren't happening as you wanted them to?

Molly:

Well, yes, I would say, every day, there's a little bit of fear, because the reality is, I own my own business now, and I can't go to my boss, I can't go to a board, or to a structure or an entity and say, "Here's what I want. Approve this. Sign this form. Notarize, this. Tell me I can do this." I'm the one that's allowing this thing to be created, so there's not this safety net if you will. And yet, with the lack of a safety net comes an incredible feeling of freedom. I don't want to go back to the systems and structures that felt really safe, because with that safety, there was not much freedom. I think you have to prioritize, or at least look at it from a healthy lens: freedom comes with fear, or you can eliminate the fear and have no freedom. Which sounds more appealing to you? For me, I can deal with a little fear. But to be a really small business owner during the global pandemic, I had no idea how that was going to play out. I had to reinvent my entire business. And I'm here and I'm okay. And my bills are paid. And I have new clients. I think so many people navigate this space thinking, well, I'll know it's good when there's no fear. And that just hasn't been my experience. Yes, there's fear. And there's freedom. And those two things for me go together. And I can live with that.

Melissa:

I'm all in on this notion that comfort is an illusion, that comfort costs us if we stick with it. In the model you've given here of fear and freedom, comfort would be in holding on to seek safety, no matter what. But even that's gonna come at a cost. Because you have no freedom, right? So comfort is always costing us. Why do people cling so much to this notion of comfort?

Molly:

To me, the mental image that comes to mind, and the one that I use a lot is that of a trapeze artist. They're holding on to this bar and they're flying through space. Every time they go forward and every time they go backward, they see this other bar flying towards them, this empty bar, and every time they have to make a decision to keep holding on or let go, keep holding on or let go. But if you choose to let go, there's going to be a moment when you hold on to nothing. Because again, to go back to that mental picture from holding onto one bar and grabbing on to the next, they would be split in half. So it's one or the other. Where's the comfort in any of that? What's comfortable is just sticking to what you know. And, I do think it's an illusion we have to keep telling ourselves, "This works for me, I like this. I've done this for 30 years, nothing has changed. This feels comfortable." But is it really comfort? Or is that all you know?

When I was leaving coaching, I felt like I was at this critical crossroads of staying with what I knew or embracing the unknown. I mean, totally unknown, like this thing I was going to create didn't have a foundation built yet. What was it going to be? And I felt like the risk of staying was greater than the risk of the unknown. One of the things I've said to a lot of people is, as they may be going through this thought process of "Do I let go? Do I embrace what's next?" is, "What's the worst-case scenario? And if you can live with the worst-case scenario, maybe you should try.

When I left coaching, I'll never forget the first three people who contacted me, it was all panic buttons, voicemails, and texts, like, "What if you're homeless? What if, what if, what if, what if, what if?" And I was like, whoa, whoa, whoa, there are a lot of steps between where I'm at right now and literally losing my house. There are many things that happen in between. For me, the worst-case scenario was, maybe I have to rent out my guest bedroom to help pay for my mortgage. Maybe I have to get a part-time job at Barnes and Noble, which would be heaven for me to spend 20 hours a week in a bookstore. That's my worst-case scenario. Can I live with that? Yes, I can.

I think it's really important that people really wrestle with what's the worst-case scenario. There's a friend of mine right now who's in the process of leaving the ministry and starting an outdoor wilderness kind of experience business, and he's got a lot of fear. And I've been asking him, "What's the worst-case scenario?" And he's like, "I go back to being an interim pastor for a couple of months." When I ask him if he can live with that? He says, "Oh, yes, I can, I can. Yes, I can live with that." Okay. I was like, Alright, let's keep going with that list. What else is worst-case scenario? He says, "I work with REI, 20 hours a week and get an employee discount. I can live with that." When you do something new and uncomfortable, you have to wrap your brain around: What's the worst-case scenario? Can you live with that?

Melissa:

How did you navigate the pitfalls?

Molly:

I think a lot of it comes back to my coaching, like, there are times when you know what the game plan is, and then your best two players get injured. Well, okay, we got to figure this out. We've got to work with what we have and come up with a strategy where we can be successful. And so

I think I leaned a lot on that approach, like, here are the puzzle pieces I have, the constraints I'm working with, let's go because come game day, you have to figure it out. And so you know, definitely my coaching background, particularly coaching in athletics, where you're just dealing with so many unknowns, what's the weather like that day? How are the officials calling the game? How are your players' bodies? How are your players' minds, all these things you can't control? And you just have to find a way. That's the same strategy applied to life as a small business owner during a global health crisis, and even in all the "ordinary" days when challenges arise.

Melissa:

Awesome. Any other thoughts you want to share on leaning into the uncomfortable stuff?

Molly:

Part of what I have shared with people is you can always go back. We forget that. I could go back to coaching today. I might have to relocate, it might not be, you know, the top 10 schools that I want, I might have to be an assistant coach. But I could go back, I don't want to go back. But I could go back. Things don't have to be final. Go try something. And if it's not for you, maybe you go back, maybe you just need to step away and see something with fresh eyes. Maybe you're better when you go back to that thing. But you can go back, assuming you're not blowing up bridges in the process.

~

What I love about Molly's story is that she fully acknowledges what's uncomfortable, and frames it in a way that encourages her. She chooses the discomfort that gives her the life and freedom she wants. Then, she made a plan, considered the cost, and took action.

Acknowledging that there is discomfort in any choice we make, and choosing the discomfort that serves us, can be a life-giving revelation. If the adversity you face centers on debt, that's uncomfortable! Living paycheck to paycheck is uncomfortable. So is budgeting and cutting out expenses. You **choose** the discomfort that leads you toward what you want in life.

Whatever struggle you face, there will be discomfort in any action you take, even (perhaps, especially) with inaction. Which discomfort will serve you best? Which discomfort gives you joy and meaning in your life? Choose which serves you best. At some point, to use Molly's metaphor, will you decide to let go of the bar you hold to grab another, or will you keep a solid grip on the bar you've held? To try both will split you down the middle. When you choose, remember that God is in the depths of your struggles. That moment when you float between the two bars, holding onto neither; that moment of floating may be the holiest in your life because the breath you draw in at that moment is full of letting go of all that has defined you, and reaching for what beckons.

Chapter 5: Find Your People

I resented having to be there. I didn't want to be there. I had a lot of work to do and attending this conference for three days would only make that list longer. That was my attitude as I stomped up the stairs, like a moody child, and into the conference room to find a seat in the back. I figured I would put in some time and then find a solid reason to cut out early and get to my long to-do list. To be honest, my list wasn't long. That's just what I told myself. It was, actually, a good time to be away for a few days. Truth? I didn't want to be there, so I nurtured a poor mindset and a bad attitude.

There was a gentleman at my church and he always had a preacher joke for me on Sundays. One of those jokes was about a church that hired a female pastor for the first time and some elders were not happy about it, but went along with the church's decision. One of the elders' traditions was to take the new pastor out for a day of fishing. To their great displeasure, when they asked this new pastor to go, she was pleased to accept their invitation. They were having a successful outing, despite themselves. The fish were biting, and she was, it turned out, pretty good company. When their stomachs reminded them of lunchtime, they realized they had forgotten their sack lunches on the shore. The pastor jumped out of the boat and ran across the lake to retrieve them. One elder hung his head and said, "You see that? She can't even swim."

Friend - I am sad to say I was just like that elder in the boat at this conference. I discounted and found fault in everything the speaker had to say. Thankfully, I kept it to myself as I nurtured my bad attitude. It is also true that everything he had to say at that conference was brilliant, life-changing, and transformational. He shared wisdom that was going to change my life and ministry forever. Mindset matters, friend. I will discuss mindset further in later chapters, but for friends at this conference who were excited about the potential of what we were learning, I would have benefitted little from the experience. However, the excitement of these friends cut through my negativity and I became present to the moment and all that it offered. I am forever grateful that I did.

The conference introduced Bowen Theory, also known as Emotional Family Systems. The gist of Emotional Family Systems is that no singular behavior or action can be understood in a vacuum. It is only fully understood within a broader context. For example, understanding why a person withdraws from intense situations cannot be understood without looking at the individual's family of origin, the family's generational patterns, and the interpersonal dynamics of the current system(s) in which the person exhibits the behavior. This is true not only of the behaviors of individuals but also of groups, churches, communities, and societies. To understand the history of our North American continent, one must also understand the dynamics of other cultures and continents that settled here. To understand why we have the reactions to stimuli that we do, we have to study the family we grew up in. To understand how a church functions, we need to understand the generations of people in that church.

This conference began a journey of learning and discovery that helped me grow as a person and a pastor. Bowen Theory teaches one *how* to make the journey of self-discovery and self-differentiation. To self-actualize, the ultimate growth goal identified by Piaget and Maslow, and necessary to reach the advanced stages of faith identified by Fowler, is at the heart of Bowen Theory. One can learn the concepts of Bowen Theory quickly, but skillfully implementing them is a lifelong pursuit. This is best accomplished with input from others who also understand systems thinking.

My dear friend and colleague, April, immediately saw the wisdom and transformational value. Her excitement kept me hooked. We traveled together throughout the Midwest and made many trips to the North Carolina mountains to be a part of a group that gathered three times a year to continue to study Bowen Theory and help each other apply its wisdom in our lives and ministries. These were the right people at the right time. We confided in each other, trusted each other, and told each other hard truths we needed to hear. I maintain relationships that were made during those years and often seek their wisdom, listen to their stories, and offer input when asked.

I have learned the importance of having the right people at the right time. The people we love most play vital roles in our lives, but they may not have the particular skills or expertise we need at the time. That's not to say we cast them aside when we don't "need" them. Please don't misunderstand. It's important to prioritize time with the people we love. However, each person you love may not have the expertise to counsel or guide you in every situation. You may need a business manager, a realtor, a doctor, a therapist, a pastor/spiritual guide, a voice coach, a designer, a contractor, etc. You may need someone who will speak the truth in love, a friend who always encourages, or the person who keeps you accountable while you navigate a season of life. That's not to say you forsake those who aren't who you need (unless they will work against you, then you may want to create some space for a time), but that you prioritize time with those who will support you in a manner you need support.

I was very young when I made a decision that would shape my well-being long into adulthood. Being the youngest child by eight years, I watched how my family interacted and noticed how each family member became stressed and anxious. I processed all of this through the eyes and limited understanding of a small child and decided (unwisely) that I would never be the source of stress or anxiety for my family. I wanted to be a source of joy and happiness.

I recall overhearing my brothers ask our parents for gas money every Friday so they could go cruising. This was the late 70s and is what we did in a small town on Friday and Saturday evenings. My parents always gave the standard parent reply, "We don't have that kind of money." It horrified me when I heard this with my "child ears," thinking that we were scary-poor and didn't even have money for gas (which was very cheap at the time) and therefore we would likely be homeless by the following week. (Dramatic much?). I did not want to be the reason we had no food or home, so when my mom would ask if I wanted to take piano lessons, I always said no, though I desperately wanted to. Again - I had decided to never stress my family.

Understand that this wasn't from any sense of altruism but from fear. I was a decade younger than my brothers and was processing what I saw and heard through the limited understanding of a small child. Had I simply confided any of this to my parents, they would have quickly cleared up my misconceptions. From the earliest age, I over-thought and over-processed. Many instances like this occurred throughout my childhood.

In deciding that I would not cause any stress or discomfort to my family, I ignored any emotions I had that were not "happy" ones. Everybody is happy when they laugh. Happy is good. Sad and anxious is bad. As you might imagine, this was a fantastic blueprint for growing into an emotionally ignorant and easily depressed adult who struggles with relationships, avoids conflict, and distracts from anxious situations by cracking jokes. When the time came for me to begin a journey of self-differentiation, it would be a very long and winding road.

Shortly after going to the conference that introduced Bowen Theory, my community experienced a collective trauma when a plastics plant at the edge of our village had an explosion. Our Village was impacted economically when the plant ceased to operate, emotionally in the wake of the deaths of those working, and spiritually as the questions of 'how could this happen to us' settled in. After this event, I experienced some mild symptoms of PTSD. Let me tell you - mild symptoms are enough! I knew I needed help. I needed to identify and express what I felt and experienced. I needed to make space for myself and be able to cultivate meaningful personal relationships. I saw a therapist and confided my feelings to the group of Family Systems friends. This group of people on the journey of self-discovery and growth I had stumbled into were exactly who I needed to help me grow.

It was a huge and terrifying moment for me the first time I expressed a genuine emotion out loud to another person, an emotion I knew would cause disruption and discomfort. Guess what? We all survived. To my utter surprise, it wasn't a big fat hairy deal to the other person, who was glad I had spoken up. I was stunned. It was an incredible discovery. It took me back to those first moments of AIT when I decided I mattered enough to struggle for. Is it possible to go through life like this? Is this how people lived - just going about life honest with themselves? I wanted to try. It's still difficult, and often I'm tempted to fall back into old and comfortable patterns of withdrawing into myself and riding out the storm. But, one cannot hold on to one bar *and* grasp the next.

In intense moments, it's challenging to honestly and articulately express what I feel, but I need to do it. You need to do it, too. It's a measure of growth when we can do this calmly and in a manner that clarifies our thoughts and emotions so that others can understand, without attacking or belittling others. The better we are at this, the more we can understand and appreciate the perspectives of others, too. Life continues to be a journey of discovery, finding my voice, and creating some elbow room. Having the right people at the right time was crucial for growth.

What struggle is in front of you? Find your people. Find the trained experts you need, the encouragers you need, the truth-tellers you need, and the comforters you need. And then love them. Cherish them. Appreciate them. Nurture them. Be present to them as they are present to you. The right people make all the difference.

Chapter 6: Manage Your Emotions

I went through the house, lighting candles. It was late and I could have gone to bed, but the loud sound had me wide awake and I sprang into action. For whatever reason, a piece of wood furniture broke and made a loud noise as it fell to the floor. My mind immediately went to thinking the power was out, so I got candles and lit them.

However...

The power was on.

The lights were on.

Every room had lights.

There were two active parts of my brain. One was frantic about gathering and lighting candles after the loud furniture crash. Another told me there was no power outage and no need to light candles. I had two realities vying for dominance in my consciousness.

The compulsion to light candles was strong, and I struggled to make sense of the other information my brain was trying to communicate. I was confused and scared. I remember standing in the middle of the living room, much like I had stood the night of the big plastics plant explosion in our village, trying to make sense of what was happening.

I *needed* to finish lighting the candles. The urge was irresistible.

The power was on.

What was happening to me?

Another thought was trying to break through. The sound of crashing furniture got me moving. I was repeating what I did the night of the plastics plant explosion... Isn't that PTSD? Suddenly, a flood of memories flashed through my consciousness: the memory of the plant explosion, the memory of nighttime earthquakes in a foreign country I had visited, scenes from AIT, news of a beloved aunt who had suddenly and unexpectedly passed away at a critical juncture in my life. Every moment in my life, when I felt vulnerable and afraid, paraded through my thoughts as my heart raced and I fought the compulsion to *JUST LIGHT THE DAMN CANDLES*.

I sat and breathed. I managed to soothe myself that evening, but I was scared. I was embarrassed. PTSD is for soldiers who have experienced atrocities. Who was I to have PTSD in my life? The next few weeks were rough. Life wasn't ok. I could function, but I was not well. At any moment, I could crumble into a ball and not be able to function at all. I felt vulnerable in a way that I had not felt before. I knew what was happening to me. I even had a name for it and a speck of knowledge about it, and I felt shame over it. Why

56

couldn't I get through it? It wasn't a severe case, as I had some awareness of the reality around me, even when I was experiencing its symptoms.

I talked to a Vietnam vet in my congregation and told him what I was experiencing. I even apologized to him for experiencing it. His grace and compassion saved my life that day. He told me what I needed to hear. He assured me I could heal from it, encouraged me to get help, and gave me a big ole bear hug and a tissue. I knew then what I needed to do and had confidence in what he told me. There was a bit of light shining in the darkness. I made an appointment with a therapist.

Many things were coming together at once: life experiences, the tribe I needed, the congregation I cherished that wanted me to be the best person and pastor I could be, a family I loved and who loved me, a growing knowledge of Emotional Family Systems, and a guiding, loving Presence directing me through it all. It was *SO* uncomfortable but rife with possibilities.

When I sat down with the therapist in the first session, she asked me what brought me that day. I responded, "Well, I would feel much less anxious sitting on a pile of lit firecrackers than expressing an emotion."

"Let's start there," she said. So, we revisited that five-year-old girl who witnessed the power of emotions and decided to opt out and withdraw into the safety of books instead. It was time to get back to my life.

I was ready. The stars aligned. I had the people I needed. I had a goal: to be aware of my emotions, be able to identify them, and then articulate that to others calmly and confidently. I began speaking a new truth to myself: I am an emotionally aware and intelligent being. I repeated that affirmation to myself daily. I began believing it and living it. I was ready for the work of learning my emotions and managing them in healthy ways.

Growth happened quickly, but not easily. I had become adept at shoving down and ignoring any powerful emotion. The unexpected death of my aunt is a perfect example. She was my mother's sister, one of five siblings, and the one everyone in our family turned to for advice, comfort, love - you name it. She was, without question, the heart of us all. News of her death spun us all out of our orbits. This happened **the day** I was moving to another state to attend seminary. A big exciting part of relocating was that I would be near her and I could visit and curl up with her any time I wanted to, and at a time that I knew I would sorely need it.

The news of her death was crippling, but I didn't have time to mourn her. I had to load my things. Saints from my church would arrive that afternoon to move me and my stuff two states away. When I arrived at my studio apartment in Lexington, KY, I moved in and unpacked. I met new people who would be companions in this spiritual boot camp called seminary. Who would want to hang out with the sad girl who mourned? No one! So I *never* mentioned it. I shoved it down with everything else, as I had become so adept at doing. It's probably no surprise that I barely functioned and experienced a major bout of depression. By some miracle, I made lifelong friends at the seminary and it's a testimony to their grace that they abided me in my emotionally cut-off and needy condition.

Only by the grace and strength of God had I made it through life mostly intact. It was no surprise that I struggled with relationships. It was time to unpack and pull out the things I had buried deeply and bring them into the light. Part of me was aware, much like how God spoke to me on that first day of AIT, that if I was going to stay in ministry and have any impact, I needed to do this work. Otherwise, I was on the fast track to washing out and becoming another ministry burnout statistic.

Friend, hear this: we are beautifully and wonderfully made. We are capable of so much. You matter. Your experience matters. If you struggle and suffer, you can heal. When you feel stranded and alone in the darkness, there is Light. You may have noticed that a few times in my experience I mentioned that I felt shame. Shame is a desperate act of darkness to keep out the Light. Shame is the jailor that keeps the keys to freedom out of reach. It is not worth clinging to. If you suffer under the grip of shame, go out and grab Brené Brown's books or watch her YouTube videos and kick shame out of your life. Know this: you are loved and cherished beyond measure by the Source of all that is light, life, and love in this world, and you can heal. You are worth the work and the effort.

A major component of getting through any adversity in your life is to manage the emotions that come with the adversity you face. You will experience "new" emotions that arise in the moment, and former and unresolved emotions. Emotions stay with us until we face them. They hang out somewhere in our bodies until we process and release them. You will know you have accomplished this when you can recall the experience from which they came, without the "gut clinch," or reliving of them.

When you are "in the grips" of the sad or difficult emotional stuff, your emotions pervade your experience. Emotions do not recognize or honor boundaries and will spill out, over, and into all areas of your life. In his book, *Man's Search For Meaning*[10], Viktor Frankl discusses his experience as a therapist. When his clients would discover

[10] Viktor Frankl, *Man's Search For Meaning,* Boston: Beacon Press, 1962.

that he was an Auschwitz survivor, they would dismiss their struggles and apologize for them. They felt their struggles were insignificant compared to his experience. He would tell them that struggle, pain, and despair were pervasive; these emotions fill a person and need/deserve to be healed.

One who pours a bucket of water over his head will get soaked. So will one who stands in the pouring rain. Each should receive a towel. As humans, we tend to judge our experiences, our conditions, and our emotions against others. This practice doesn't help us and leads us to trivialize or inflate them. Our experiences belong to us. Our emotions are our responsibility to heal. Healing them is to process and release them.

Chapter 7: Adopt a Relevant and Healthy Mindset

Eleanor Roosevelt, First Lady of the United States March 4, 1933- April 12, 1945, is my role model and heroine. Fearlessly pursuing what was right and just, she did not care what anyone thought of her. She used her influence to fight for civil rights legislation for African and Asian Americans and women's rights. She went a step further and advocated for the full inclusion in decision-making roles for all. Eleanor was a pioneer First Lady, redefining her traditional role into one where she could further the well-being of all Americans. She openly disagreed with her husband on some issues and represented him in the United States and abroad when he couldn't go himself. She wrote a daily newspaper column, spoke on a daily radio show, and often spoke at live events. All the above actions were unheard of for a woman, and especially for the First Lady of the United States.[11]

Following her husband's death, she continued her political life. She pushed the United States to join the United Nations and became its first delegate. She was the inaugural

---

[11] Evans, Erin, and Erin Evans Believer in mindfulness. "31 Inspiring Eleanor Roosevelt Quotes." Bright Drops, May 26, 2021. https://brightdrops.com/eleanor-roosevelt-quotes.

Chair of the Commission on Human Rights and led the drafting of the Universal Declaration of Human Rights. During her long career, she gained worldwide esteem.

Given her career and achievements, many of her quotes still inspire. Here are a few of my favorites:

"People grow through experience if they meet life honestly and courageously."

"I am what I am today because of the choices I made yesterday."

"You must do things you think you cannot do."

"It is better to light a candle than curse the darkness."

"I believe anyone can conquer fear by doing the things he (sic) fears to do."

"No one can make you feel inferior without your consent."

"What one has to do usually can be done."

"Never allow a person to tell you no who doesn't have the power to say yes."

"In the long run, we shape our lives and we shape ourselves."

"You can often change your circumstances by changing your attitude."

"With the new day comes new strength and new thoughts."[12]

These quotes stand out because they concern one's mindset toward a problem or challenge. The importance of one's mindset while working through something difficult or impossible cannot be overstated. Resilience and perseverance play key roles in overcoming obstacles and mindset fuels both.

I cannot recall an example of when I was "all in" on a problem and came up short. When I failed, I can see that my mindset was not aligned with my actions. Mindset matters.

A student of the Bible might recall many instances encouraging us to have a good mindset. Here are a few examples:

In Mark chapter 9, we read the story about how Jesus and three of his disciples went up a mountain and experienced the definition of a mountaintop moment. Jesus transfigured, meaning he turned dazzling white and glowed supernaturally. Moses and Elijah, long-past Biblical figures, appeared with him. Jesus, Moses, and Elijah spoke while the three disciples tried to understand what they saw. It was a mind-blowing experience that the three disciples wouldn't fully understand until after Jesus' resurrection.

---

[12] Ibid.

I cannot imagine what was happening in their hearts and minds as they descended the mountain. I'm sure they had a pretty good idea about who Jesus was by this point, but knowing is one thing; experiencing it is another matter.

I recall a similar moment, myself. Nothing glowed supernaturally and Moses and Elijah didn't attend, but it was a holy moment. It was Christmas Eve and my brothers and I were all home to celebrate the holidays. As was our custom, we finished a sumptuous family feast and then went to our family church for the traditional candlelight Communion service. Near the end of the service, we all stood in a circle and shared Communion. Then we sang Silent Night and the light from the Christ candle was passed around, each person lighting the candle of the person next to them until everyone in the circle held a lighted candle. After we proclaimed the joy of Christ's birth, we received a blessing and a call to go and share the joyous news with others.

As we circled the dimmed sanctuary, illuminated by the Light of Christ, I felt a Presence like none other I have felt before or since. I struggle to articulate what I felt, knew, and experienced, but it was beyond an earthly experience. I felt the embrace of God. It was a warm love - so strong, pure, and inviting - it would change my life. Leaving that sanctuary, I was a new person, encountering holiness in a way I never had previously. That holy encounter took me from a posture of **believing** in God to one of **knowing** God. I carry that memory with me. It comforts, inspires and awakens me. I want it again. My spirit craves it, and there's nothing I wouldn't give up, set aside, or overcome to have it.

Having that experience, I still cannot imagine what was going through the three disciples' hearts and minds as they descended the mountain after seeing Jesus in all his glory. Of course, as it is wont to do, life breaks in. A big melee had broken out around a guy who brought his son to the other disciples to heal. He was afraid for his son's life, and wanted Jesus to heal him from whatever had hold of him, *if he was able.* In verse twenty-three, Jesus exclaims to him and all the others around that *all things* are possible to those who believe. When I read this, I picture the three disciples who had been with Jesus on the mountain, nodding their agreement.

Jesus told the desperate father that he needed to change his mindset. In the short exchange that followed, the man acknowledged this and that he needed Jesus' help to do it. The man's mindset was a critical element in his son's healing.

Jesus said this another way in his Sermon on the Mount. Matthew records this epic event in which Jesus preaches and teaches to a large crowd for an extended time. In it, he covers a lot of spiritual fundamentals. Much of his teaching surprised and amazed those who heard, as his message turned conventional wisdom on its head. He invited them to have another view of God, life and themselves. He invited them to change their mindset.

Jesus often used the phrase, "let those with eyes to see," or the similar phrase, "let those with ears to hear." When he used those phrases, he was encouraging his listeners to have a different mindset regarding what they knew, or thought they knew, about faith.

Paul, who wrote much of the New Testament, also spoke about the importance of mindset. In his letter to the Philippians, he encouraged them to:

"Adopt the same attitude as that of Christ Jesus," (Phil 2:5 CSB)

In his letter to the Romans, he said:

"For those who live according to the flesh have their minds set on the things of the flesh, but those who live according to the Spirit have their minds set on the things of the Spirit." (Rom 8:5 CSB)

And later in chapter 12 he said:

"Do not be conformed to this age, but be transformed by the renewing of your mind, so that you may discern what is the good, pleasing, and perfect will of God." (Rom 12:2 CSB)

These are but a few of the many times the Biblical giants exhort us to have the right mindset to live and grow in faith.

Friends, our mindset is the fuel for living. Without the right mindset, we will sputter and stall. With the right mindset, we can overcome more than we ever thought possible. Whatever it is you are going through, whatever has your stomach tied in knots, and your mind racing instead of sleeping; cultivating an appropriate mindset is a huge chunk of the struggle.

This begs the question then of how does one cultivate a mindset that allows for growth? It begins with the fundamental and intentional choice to do so supported by the belief that you are worth the effort. I remember, with absolute clarity, the moment in AIT when I made the choice to overcome. In that moment, I also acknowledged that I was a human, fearfully and wonderfully made, and deserving of the life my choices would bring. My future was worth the struggle. Without that foundational belief in my worth, I wouldn't have had the strength and fuel to do the necessary work.

Start there. Dearest - you are worth the struggle. You are a human that was fearfully and wonderfully made. You deserve the future you choose and work to bring forth. (I mean, don't work to be a jerk.) Work to grow and bring good into the world. If you cannot do this yourself, find someone to help you. Wake up each morning with this belief. If you've been told, as many have, by parents or other authorities that you are not worth a dang, I am here to tell you they are wrong. Flat wrong. Not buts, no exceptions. There's redemption for everyone. Yes, even for you. Especially for you. Jesus says so, and I don't know a higher authority than that.

Now you are ready to build on the foundation of self-belief. There's a lot you can do to create a strong and positive mindset that will serve you in the struggle that's in front of you and beyond. Surround yourself with positive messages. This may require changing the media you consume and the people you listen to. Immerse yourself in positive climates, and bonus points if this climate is also moving toward the same goal you are.

In my biology studies, I took a class on neurobiology. In it, I remember learning that sleep is vital to wiring memories and experiences into our brains long term. The structures and processes that accomplish this long-term wiring decide what is important to encode and what should not be encoded by tossing some of the day's thoughts into the "keep" pile and tossing the rest into the "wastebasket" as you sleep. How is the sorting of info decided? The deciding factor is how much time you spend thinking your thoughts during your waking hours. When we think, chemical stuff happens in our brains and makes neural connections. The more connections, the more import the info. This freaks me out a bit (a lot) because I can spend loads of time thinking about things that I don't want in my permanent brain file. The important consequence to consider is to focus our minds on what we want long term. Thus, it's important to surround yourself with positive messaging that supports you. (Side note - this also is how social media and ad-driven search works: we see more of the things we click on.)

We can fortify our brains with affirmations. Affirmations are powerful tools. Think of affirmations as vital nutrients you need each day. One I use often is, "I can do hard things." When I get frustrated, I take a breath and repeat this to myself. It helps. A simple online search will give you a bunch of affirmations you can use. I like to make them specific to what I am trying to accomplish. If you are wanting to be better at making presentations, for example, you might write an affirmation for yourself such as, "I am a capable and intelligent professional. I know how to communicate information and inspire others." Find or write affirmations that work for you. These are positive statements that reflect the goal before you. Do not write to avoid the negative, but to reinforce the positive. In the above example, a poor affirmation would be, "I won't panic and forget my main points." That's not helpful, because it brings the negative thought to mind. Instead, write or say, "I am calm and know my content well."

Fill your brain with affirmations. Write them in your journal. Say them to yourself. Record yourself saying them and play that recording in your car or listen to it on your phone. The idea is to have the thoughts hard-wired into your consciousness. The more you think about it, the more it will be real. This applies to the messaging we receive from affirmations, media, personal conversations, and all the things that enter our thoughts. Choose what you want to keep and endeavor to hear those messages and "think" them into your brain.

Gratitude is a spiritual "superfood." Gratitude brings our focus to what is present to us and away from what we lack. It helps us to recognize what is important and prioritize what we want more of in our lives. I do not have hard data, and can't give you any statistics about the difference gratitude makes in people's lives. However, I can share what

I've seen in twenty-five plus years of ministry. People who are grateful enjoy life a heck of a lot more than people who aren't. I've seen people who have ample finances, health, and opportunities have a miserable outlook on life. I have also seen people who live with a lot less enjoy their life and make the most of what's available to them. Sometimes people tell me they feel "stuck." When they want advice, I prescribe practicing gratitude and doing something in service to others as methods to get out of neutral. Speaking of which, volunteer somewhere. Volunteer for an afternoon, or make it an ongoing commitment. Serving others awakens us to a belief in our innate abilities, gratitude for what we have, and a spiritual presence abiding with within us. All good things when we are working to overcome a difficult season of life.

To form a mindset that serves you, add the word 'yet' to your vocabulary. Whenever you call to mind a fault, add the word yet. Instead of saying, "I'm not good at (fill in the blank)," or "I can't (fill in the blank)," say, "I'm not good at (fill in the blank) yet." Or, "I can't (fill in the blank) yet." This subtle shift leads to different thoughts and beliefs. These new thoughts and beliefs about ourselves lead to new actions. These new actions lead to new results. If you *want* something different, you have to *do* something different.

A mindset that serves you in forming the life you want is critical. Sometimes, a mindset change alone can be what we need to get us over the obstacle in front of us. Take the time to ensure you are cultivating a good mindset in your life. Break the habits that work against you. Form new habits that feed and nurture your body, mind, and spirit. Make subtle changes that lead to healthy actions. Step by step, you will see a change in your views and beliefs about your capabilities. You may also notice a growth in compassion for others.

My friend Julie champions mindset in her life.

"I remember making a decision that day that I was going to have to say what I needed to say and ask for what I needed to have because there was no one else to do it for me."

Julie is an only parent to her teenage daughter. Already feeling the heavy weight of responsibility weighing on her, she walked into the hospital for a bone biopsy. It was Friday the 13th, also Good Friday, in March 2020. More profoundly, it was also the day the governor shut down all non-essentials in her state due to the COVID pandemic. Julie was alone to face the events awaiting her inside the hospital doors. No parent, friend, pastor, or chaplain could go with her. The words above echoed in her mind as she reached to open the doors.

A bone biopsy requires removing bone marrow to analyze, which involves drilling into the bone to retrieve the marrow. This procedure involved some emotional preparation and steel. Julie was utterly overwhelmed. She knew what she could handle and what she could not, and this was something she could not. She tearfully confided this to the nurse preparing her for her procedure. With this knowledge, staff adjusted her care.

I have long admired Julie and the way she carries herself through life. She creates the mindset she needs to see her through whatever challenge lies in front of her, even when she has to take life moment by moment. Having a mindset that supported her enabled her to get through a terrifying experience.

Conclusion: Coming Full-Circle

"Bulls**t!"

"No way those are threes!"

My brother's expression told us all we needed to know.

To anyone else, it's a cardgame requiring a lot of bluffing and calling each other out on their bluffs. To us, it was a healing balm. My brothers and I, and our families, sat around a table playing a silly game of cards that didn't require much thinking or strategy because we didn't have it in us. We buried our mother earlier that day. Friends and family had gone home, and we were left to ourselves. Our father died thirteen years ago. We're a smaller group now, minus one - the big one - the one who brought us into the world. The one who connected us to the generation before and, along with our father, raised us and passed on the traditions of a time gone by. We were sad. We were grieving. We were also hopeful. We did what we were always taught to do: make the most of the moment we're in. For us, that meant shuffling a deck of cards and taunting the ones we love most.

At eighteen I took my first stand and found my strength. That action, and the inner growth that came with it, continue to provide me courage and direction. As I sat with my family and called out their bluffs and made a few of my own, I recalled many of the gifts our mom passed down to us. I thought about a story she told me when she was a teenager and was repeatedly threatened by her stepmother. In an incredible act of courage, when her stepmother "came at her again in the kitchen," Mom grabbed a butcher's knife and told her, "Stop! This ends now. Either you stop, or I will stop you." I cannot begin to imagine the events that led to that encounter, or the courage she had to summon to stand her ground that day. But I do know that it was a defining moment for her, and undergirded many future actions she would take in her life. I like to think that her act of courage inspires my own, and the stand I took at eighteen in AIT continues the tradition of facing my problems head-on.

My parents never let difficult times define them. They faced them however they could and came through to the other side. They modeled courage and integrity to us as they navigated life together.

I'm still growing into these lessons. At times, when I'm afraid to confront or to get through a scary and overwhelming time, I take a breath and remember from whence I came. I recall my own experiences. I remember that the quickest way to remove these problems from my present and place them into my past is to plot a path straight through and get on with it. Time spent worrying and fretting is time added to the struggle.

Losing my mother has brought me full circle. A week following the funeral I was back in my two churches. We wept together, and I wasn't afraid of my tears. I have known and loved these folks for decades, and I need them. They need me to be authentically present. At that time, my authentic presence was vulnerable and grieving.

For perhaps the first time in my life, I was okay being so vulnerable and I was able to ask them for what I needed to heal. I needed a sabbatical. A semi-sabbatical, actually. I didn't want to be apart from them, because I needed them and their support and compassion to heal. I also needed to not be a pastor for a while. I asked for 10 weeks off, but wanting to preach on Sundays. Basically, I asked to simply be a supply preacher for the summer with no other responsibilieties, and to return fully after Labor Day. They graciously agreed I needed it and granted it on the spot.

I knew how easy it would be to succumb to the old familiar pull of checking out emotionally and to give in to the comforts of avoidance. It would be so easy to get lost online, scroll on my phone late into the night and sleep well into the day. The pull was there... it would be so easy to give into it. However, that is not the life I want, so I sat down and scratched out a map to follow that has served me well over the years.

My Plan:

- Create healthy habits and daily routines for my body mind and spirit.
- Spend time with my brothers and devise a plan for staying connected to each other now that our "Home Base" is gone.
- Do some fun things!
- Visit friends.
- Disconnect digitally - no social media, make new habits using my devices less.
- Go to bed by 10:30 PM and rise at 6:30 AM.
- Be honest when people ask how I'm doing. Outside of worship, I plan to wear no makeup. Tears will come when they come, and I will NOT apologize for them.

My People:

- Family: deepen connections with my brothers, and be "all in" at family gatherings this summer.
- Friends: I want to reconnect with friends in ministry.

- Spiritual Guide: I want to ensure I'm focused, centered, and rooted in the Divine, and open to new ways of connecting.

Emotions I Need to Process:

- Sorrow: thankfully, I only have sorrow and not despair or anger. I'm grateful for this, as sorrow is enough. The loss of my parents was sad, but not tragic, and there was no unfinished emotional business or injustice in their deaths. We dealt with conflict and misunderstandings throughout our lives together as they arose. I'm so thankful they modeled that and taught us how to live it.

- Depression: I feel emptiness, but not discouragement. In fact, the grace of my churches *en*courages me to face the emptiness and know that I am loved and cared for by God and many others. The red flags of depression are certainly present and it would be so easy to give into the old pull of disconnecting from my emotions, but I don't want that life again. To process this grief and the reality of a new stage of life without parents, I need to set strict boundaries: Each day I need to set an alarm for

6:30 AM and get out of bed. I need to accomplish something each morning, like a household task, or workout, or something else. I need to eat well, move each day - especially if I don't want to - and put my phone down and go to bed at 10:30. I have learned that these actions are the key for me to resist the pull of disconnecting and sliding into depression.

Mindset:
- I can do difficult things.
- I can heal from grief.
- I can make new habits.
- I can care for my body, mind, and spirit.
- I can connect with people I love.
- I can survive difficult days.
- I can create strategies to overcome obstacles.

A solid plan, gathering my people, processing my emotions, and adopting a relevant and healthy mindset are the cornerstones that have brought me through this life and into the embrace of a loving God. I continue to build on them, now and in the future, to create a life I love. They enable me to overcome the yucky stuff life throws my way, navigate the difficult times, and grow an ever-stronger connection with myself, others, and with the God I know and love - and who knows and loves me. I've experienced the strength of these cornerstones as I navigate through life, and I have witnessed their power in the lives of countless others over the years as well.

My wish for you, dear reader, is to embark on your own journey of growth without letting the heartache, the obstacles, the injustices - or anything else that would stop you from growing - derail you from your sacred journey. The path can be long and rife with uncomfortable truths and challenges, but there's no better journey to take. In the words of St. Julian, "All shall be well, all shall be well, and all manner of things shall be well." Ultimately, eternally, you will be well, too.

www.ingramcontent.com/pod-product-compliance
Lightning Source LLC
Chambersburg PA
CBHW071535120626
46550CB00006B/2465